The Expression of Emotions VOCABULARY:

What Your Feelings Are Trying to Communicate

Chris Wilton

Table of contents

INTRODUCTION

The Expression of Emotions: What Your Feelings Are Trying to Communicate," learn the secret language of your emotions.

Have you ever questioned why humans are capable of such a wide range of emotions? What if our emotions were a powerful form of communication rather than merely random fluctuations? We dig into the complex realm of emotions in this enthralling inquiry and reveal the potent signals they convey.
Come along on an illuminating trip with us as we explore the complexities of happiness, sadness, rage, love, and everything in between. Our emotions are the vivid colors that paint the canvas of our existence, from the small hints to the powerful waves.

You'll learn more about your emotional state through perceptive stories, empirical research, and useful strategies.

Understanding emotional cues: Exploring how emotions manifest through facial expressions, body language, tone of voice, and other nonverbal signals.

CHAPTER 1

EMOTIONAL INTELLIGENCE

Emotional intelligence refers to the ability to recognize, understand, and manage emotions, both in oneself and in others. It encompasses a set of skills that enable individuals to navigate social interactions, build relationships, and make sound decisions based on emotional cues. Recognizing and developing emotional intelligence is crucial for personal growth, effective communication, and success in various areas of life, including work, relationships, and overall well-being.

One aspect of emotional intelligence is self-awareness, which involves recognizing and understanding one's own emotions, strengths, weaknesses, and values. By being aware of our emotions, we gain insight into how they influence our thoughts, behaviors, and decision-making processes. This self-awareness helps us to better manage our emotional responses and regulate our behavior in different situations. It also enables us to understand how our emotions affect others and the dynamics of interpersonal relationships.

Understanding the emotions of others is another important aspect of emotional intelligence. This skill, known as empathy, involves the ability to perceive and understand the emotions, perspectives, and experiences of other people. Empathy allows us to connect with others on a deeper level, showing compassion, and providing support when needed. By understanding the emotions of others, we can communicate more effectively, resolve conflicts, and build stronger relationships based on trust and mutual understanding.

Managing emotions, both our own and those of others, is a critical skill in emotional intelligence. It involves the ability to regulate and control our emotional responses in different situations. This means being able to manage stress, handle frustration, and bounce back from setbacks. Emotionally intelligent individuals can express their emotions appropriately, assertively, and constructively, without causing harm to themselves or others. They are also skilled at helping others manage their emotions, providing comfort, and offering solutions when needed.

Recognizing, understanding, and managing emotions have numerous benefits. Firstly, emotional intelligence promotes self-awareness and personal growth, allowing individuals to identify their strengths and weaknesses and work towards self-improvement. It also helps individuals navigate social interactions more effectively, as they are better able to interpret non-verbal cues, understand others' perspectives, and adjust their communication style accordingly. In professional settings, emotional intelligence is highly valued, as it contributes to effective leadership, teamwork, and conflict resolution. It also enhances decision-making abilities, as emotions play a significant role in the choices we make.

Moreover, emotional intelligence contributes to mental and emotional well-being. By recognizing and managing emotions, individuals can reduce stress, anxiety, and negative emotions, leading to improved overall mental health. It also enables individuals to build healthier and more fulfilling relationships, both personally and professionally.

In conclusion, emotional intelligence plays a vital role in our lives by helping us recognize, understand, and manage emotions. Developing emotional intelligence skills allows for improved self-awareness, empathy towards others, and effective emotion regulation. It enhances communication, fosters stronger relationships, and promotes personal and professional success. Therefore, recognizing the importance of emotional intelligence and actively working to cultivate it can lead to a more fulfilling and balanced life.

CHAPTER 2

EMOTIONAL VOCABULARY

Having a rich emotional vocabulary is crucial for accurately labeling and articulating one's feelings. It refers to the ability to identify and express a wide range of emotions with specific and nuanced terms. While emotions are a fundamental aspect of human experience, many people struggle to find the right words to describe their feelings. However, developing an extensive emotional vocabulary offers several benefits.

Firstly, having a diverse emotional vocabulary allows for greater self-awareness. When we can pinpoint and label our emotions precisely, we gain a deeper understanding of ourselves and our experiences. Instead of feeling a general sense of unease, for example, we can recognize that we are experiencing anxiety or restlessness. This awareness enables us to address our emotions more effectively and take appropriate actions to manage or cope with them.

Additionally, a rich emotional vocabulary facilitates effective communication. Emotions play a significant role in our interactions with others, and being able to express our feelings accurately enhances our ability to connect and empathize with them. When we can articulate our emotions, we can convey our needs, concerns, and desires more clearly, leading to better understanding and support from others. It also enables us to engage in meaningful conversations about emotions, promoting emotional intelligence and strengthening relationships.

Furthermore, having a varied emotional vocabulary enables us to differentiate between similar emotions. For instance, instead of simply feeling "sad," we may be able to identify if we are feeling melancholy, disappointed, or grieving. This specificity helps us to address the root cause of our emotions and find appropriate coping strategies. It also allows us to recognize the subtle differences in the emotions of others, enhancing our empathy and understanding in social interactions.

A rich emotional vocabulary also helps to prevent emotional suppression or repression. When we lack the words to express our emotions, we may struggle to acknowledge and validate them. This can lead to suppressing or ignoring our feelings, which can be detrimental to our mental and emotional well-being. On the other hand, when we have a wide range of emotional terms at our disposal, we can more easily validate and accept our emotions, fostering a healthier relationship with them.

In conclusion, developing a rich emotional vocabulary is essential for accurately labeling and articulating our feelings. It enhances self-awareness, improves communication, enables differentiation between similar emotions, and prevents emotional suppression. By expanding our emotional vocabulary, we empower ourselves to better understand, express, and navigate our emotions, leading to improved emotional intelligence and overall well-being.

CHAPTER 3

EMOTIONAL LITERACY

Emotional literacy refers to the development of skills that enable individuals to interpret, comprehend, and effectively navigate their own and others' emotional states. It encompasses a deeper understanding of emotions, their triggers, and the ability to manage and respond to them appropriately. Emotional literacy goes beyond simply recognizing and labeling emotions; it involves understanding the underlying causes, expressing emotions in a healthy manner, and empathizing with the emotions of others.

One aspect of emotional literacy is self-awareness. It involves the ability to recognize and understand one's own emotions, including their intensity, triggers, and patterns. Self-awareness allows individuals to identify the emotions they are experiencing, connect them to specific events or situations, and understand how they impact their thoughts, behaviors, and overall well-being. It helps individuals become more in tune with their emotional needs and enables them to respond to their emotions in a constructive and balanced way.

Another important aspect of emotional literacy is empathy. Empathy involves the capacity to understand and share the feelings of others. It goes beyond sympathy and requires actively putting oneself in another person's shoes and comprehending their emotional experiences. Developing empathy allows individuals to connect with others on a deeper level, recognize their emotional needs, and respond in a supportive and compassionate manner. It fosters stronger relationships, effective communication, and a sense of shared understanding.

Furthermore, emotional literacy encompasses the ability to manage and regulate emotions effectively. This involves recognizing and understanding the triggers that evoke specific emotional responses and implementing strategies to manage and control those emotions. Emotional regulation enables individuals to respond to challenging situations in a more calm and collected manner, make sound decisions based on their emotions, and maintain emotional well-being. It also involves developing healthy coping mechanisms and stress management techniques to navigate difficult emotions effectively.

Cultivating emotional literacy has several benefits. Firstly, it contributes to personal growth and self-improvement. By developing a deeper understanding of one's emotions, individuals can make informed choices, set healthy boundaries, and work towards achieving emotional balance and well-being. It also enhances self-confidence and resilience, as individuals become better equipped to navigate and adapt to various emotional challenges.

Moreover, emotional literacy enhances interpersonal relationships. When individuals have a better understanding of their own emotions, they can communicate their needs and feelings more effectively to others. They are also more attuned to the emotional states of others and can respond with empathy and support. This fosters stronger connections, trust, and collaboration in personal and professional relationships.

In educational settings, emotional literacy is increasingly recognized as an essential skill. Teaching emotional literacy helps students develop emotional intelligence, social skills, and empathy, leading to improved academic performance, positive classroom environments, and better conflict resolution.

In summary, emotional literacy is crucial for interpreting, comprehending, and effectively navigating one's own and others' emotional states. By developing skills in self-awareness, empathy, and emotional regulation, individuals can enhance their personal growth, strengthen relationships, and achieve overall emotional well-being. It is a skill set that benefits individuals in various aspects of life, allowing them to lead more fulfilling and emotionally healthy lives.

Emotional literacy also plays a significant role in the realm of mental health. By developing the skills to interpret and comprehend emotions, individuals can better understand the underlying factors contributing to their mental well-being. Emotional literacy allows individuals to identify emotional triggers, patterns, and potential sources of distress. This awareness is crucial for seeking appropriate support, whether through therapy, counseling, or self-care practices. It empowers individuals to communicate their emotional experiences to mental health professionals and actively participate in their own healing and recovery processes.

Additionally, emotional literacy helps to promote emotional resilience. When individuals possess a strong foundation in understanding and managing emotions, they are better equipped to cope with stress, adversity, and life's challenges. They can develop effective strategies for self-care, stress management, and problem-solving. Emotional resilience enables individuals to bounce back from setbacks, adapt to change, and maintain a positive outlook even in difficult circumstances.

Furthermore, emotional literacy is closely tied to effective communication and conflict resolution. When individuals are skilled in interpreting and expressing their emotions, they can articulate their needs, boundaries, and concerns in a clear and assertive manner. This helps to prevent misunderstandings, fosters healthy boundaries, and contributes to the resolution of conflicts in a constructive manner. By understanding the emotions of others and practicing empathy, individuals can also navigate disagreements and negotiations with greater understanding and mutual respect.

In the professional sphere, emotional literacy is increasingly recognized as a valuable skill set. It contributes to effective leadership, teamwork, and collaboration. Leaders who possess emotional literacy can understand and respond to the needs and motivations of their team members, fostering a positive work environment and enhancing productivity. Furthermore, emotional literacy is crucial in customer service roles, where the ability to empathize and connect with clients' emotions can lead to improved customer satisfaction and loyalty.

In conclusion, emotional literacy is a fundamental skill set that encompasses the ability to interpret, comprehend, and effectively navigate one's own and others' emotional states. By developing this skill, individuals can enhance their self-awareness, empathy, emotional regulation, and communication skills. Emotional literacy contributes to personal growth, mental health, resilience, and successful interpersonal relationships. It is a skill set that holds value in various aspects of life, promoting overall well-being and fostering positive connections with oneself and others.

CHAPTER 4

EMOTIONAL SIGNALS AND NEEDS

Emotions serve as powerful signals that communicate our inner states and provide valuable information about our needs and desires. Each emotion carries a unique message and reflects a specific underlying need or motivation. Understanding and interpreting these emotional signals is key to gaining insight into ourselves and others, fostering self-awareness, and promoting effective communication and fulfillment of our needs.

When we experience emotions, they act as signals that something within us is being activated or triggered. For example, feeling anger may signal that we perceive a threat or injustice, while joy may indicate a sense of fulfillment or positive experiences. By paying attention to these emotional signals, we can begin to uncover the underlying needs and desires that drive our emotions.

Emotional signals can manifest in various ways, including physiological changes, facial expressions, body language, and verbal and non-verbal cues. For instance, a clenched fist, raised voice, or increased heart rate may accompany feelings of anger, indicating a need for fairness, respect, or autonomy. On the other hand, a smile, relaxed posture, or a light-hearted tone of voice may accompany feelings of joy, reflecting a need for connection, pleasure, or achievement.

To effectively decode emotional signals, it is essential to cultivate self-awareness and emotional intelligence. Self-awareness involves recognizing and acknowledging our own emotions, understanding their triggers, and connecting them to our underlying needs and desires. By reflecting on our emotional experiences, we can identify patterns, recurring themes, and the specific needs that drive our emotions. This self-reflection allows us to respond to our needs more effectively and make choices that align with our values and well-being.

Similarly, understanding the emotional signals of others requires empathy and active listening. Empathy involves putting ourselves in someone else's shoes, seeking to understand their emotions, and recognizing the needs and desires behind those emotions. It involves observing verbal and non-verbal cues, asking open-ended questions, and creating a safe and non-judgmental space for the other person to express themselves. By empathizing with others and recognizing their emotional signals, we can build deeper connections, improve relationships, and respond to their needs more effectively.

By uncovering the underlying needs and desires behind emotions, we can address them more directly and constructively. For example, if we recognize that our feelings of frustration stem from a need for autonomy or recognition, we can take steps to assert our boundaries or seek acknowledgment. Similarly, when we understand that someone else's anger is driven by a need for fairness or understanding, we can engage in open dialogue, actively listen, and work towards finding mutually beneficial solutions.

In summary, emotions act as powerful signals that convey our inner states and reveal the underlying needs and desires behind them. By paying attention to these emotional signals, cultivating self-awareness, and practicing empathy, we can gain valuable insights into ourselves and others. This understanding allows us to respond to our own needs more effectively, communicate our emotions and desires more authentically, and foster stronger connections and relationships. Recognizing and honoring our emotional signals is a vital step in promoting personal growth, fulfilling relationships, and overall well-being.

CHAPTER 5

EMOTIONAL EXPRESSION ACROSS CULTURES

Emotional expression varies across cultures, reflecting the diverse ways in which emotions are understood, valued, and communicated. Different cultural contexts shape the norms, rules, and expectations surrounding emotional expression, leading to variations in how emotions are displayed, interpreted, and responded to.

One important aspect of emotional expression across cultures is the display rules. Display rules refer to the cultural norms and expectations regarding when, where, and how emotions should be expressed. Some cultures encourage open and direct expression of emotions, while others emphasize restraint and control. For example, in certain Western cultures, such as the United States, expressing emotions like happiness or enthusiasm openly is generally accepted and even encouraged. In contrast, cultures influenced by Confucian traditions, such as many East Asian cultures, tend to value emotional restraint and consider emotional displays in public as inappropriate.

Cultural variations also exist in the understanding and interpretation of specific emotions. While basic emotions like happiness, sadness, anger, fear, and surprise are recognized across cultures, the way they are experienced and expressed can differ. For instance, the concept of "personal space" and the appropriate level of physical contact during emotional interactions can vary greatly between cultures. In some cultures, people may engage in close physical proximity and physical touch to express comfort or empathy, while in others, maintaining a certain distance is the norm.

Furthermore, the value placed on specific emotions can vary across cultures. In some cultures, certain emotions may be highly valued and considered integral to personal well-being and social interactions. For instance, collectivist cultures may place a strong emphasis on emotions like gratitude, respect, and loyalty as key to maintaining harmonious relationships and social cohesion. On the other hand, individualistic cultures may prioritize emotions such as personal achievement, independence, and assertiveness.

Cultural differences in emotional expression can also impact communication styles and interpersonal relationships. In high-context cultures, where non-verbal cues and contextual factors are significant, emotions may be conveyed more implicitly, relying on indirect language and subtle non-verbal signals. In low-context cultures, where direct and explicit communication is valued, emotions may be expressed more overtly through explicit statements and explicit displays of emotions.

It is important to recognize and respect cultural variations in emotional expression to avoid misunderstandings and promote effective communication. Being aware of cultural differences allows for greater empathy and understanding when interacting with individuals from different cultural backgrounds. It requires a willingness to learn and adapt to different norms and expectations surrounding emotional expression, and to approach emotional experiences with curiosity and an open mind.

In conclusion, emotional expression varies across cultures due to differences in display rules, interpretations of specific emotions, and the value placed on emotions within a cultural context. Understanding and respecting these cultural variations are crucial for effective cross-cultural communication, building meaningful relationships, and promoting cultural sensitivity and inclusivity. Recognizing that emotional expression is influenced by cultural norms allows us to appreciate the richness and diversity of human emotions across different cultural contexts.

CHAPTER 6

EMOTIONAL REGULATION AND SELF-CARE

Emotional regulation and self-care are essential for effectively managing and expressing emotions in healthy and constructive ways. Here are some strategies to help in these areas:

Self-Awareness: Develop self-awareness by paying attention to your emotions and their triggers. Notice the physical sensations, thoughts, and behaviors associated with different emotions. Understanding how emotions manifest in your body and mind is the first step in regulating and expressing them effectively.

Mindfulness and Meditation: Practice mindfulness and meditation to cultivate a non-judgmental awareness of your emotions. Regular mindfulness practice can help you observe your emotions without immediately reacting to them, allowing you to respond more intentionally and thoughtfully.

Identify and Label Emotions: Learn to accurately identify and label your emotions. Use a rich emotional vocabulary to articulate what you are feeling. This clarity enables you to better understand and communicate your emotional experiences.

Validate Your Emotions: Accept and validate your emotions without judgment. Recognize that all emotions are valid and serve a purpose. Avoid suppressing or denying your emotions, as this can lead to further distress. Instead, acknowledge and honor your feelings, allowing yourself to experience and process them.

Healthy Coping Strategies: Develop a toolbox of healthy coping strategies that help regulate and express your emotions. This can include activities such as exercise, journaling, deep breathing exercises, engaging in hobbies, or seeking social support. Find what works best for you and incorporate these strategies into your daily routine.

Self-Care Practices: Prioritize self-care to promote emotional well-being. Engage in activities that nurture and recharge you, such as getting enough sleep, maintaining a balanced diet, engaging in relaxation techniques, and engaging in activities that bring you joy and fulfillment.

Social Support: Seek support from trusted friends, family members, or mental health professionals. Sharing your emotions with others can provide perspective, validation, and guidance. Surround yourself with a supportive network that allows you to express your emotions without judgment.

Boundaries: Set healthy boundaries to protect your emotional well-being. Clearly communicate your needs, limits, and expectations in relationships and situations. Establishing boundaries helps create a safe space for expressing and managing your emotions.

Emotional Regulation Techniques: Learn and practice specific techniques for regulating your emotions, such as deep breathing exercises, progressive muscle relaxation, or guided imagery. These techniques can help you calm down, reduce stress, and regain emotional balance.

Seek Professional Help: If you find it challenging to manage or express your emotions effectively, consider seeking support from a mental health professional. They can provide guidance, teach coping skills, and help you develop personalized strategies for emotional regulation and self-care.

Remember that emotional regulation and self-care are ongoing processes. It takes time and practice to develop these skills effectively. Be patient with yourself, and approach your emotions with kindness and compassion. With consistent effort and a commitment to your emotional well-being, you can cultivate healthier and more constructive ways of managing and expressing your emotions.

CHAPTER 7

EMPATHY AND CONNECTION

Empathy is the ability to understand and share the feelings of others. It plays a crucial role in fostering deeper connections and improving relationships. When we empathize with others, we step into their shoes, strive to understand their emotions, and validate their experiences. This empathetic response creates a sense of connection, trust, and mutual understanding, which are the foundations of healthy and meaningful relationships.

Here's how empathy and understanding others' emotions can enhance connections and relationships:

Emotional Validation: When we validate someone's emotions, we acknowledge and accept their feelings as valid and understandable. This validation helps individuals feel heard, seen, and understood. It communicates that their emotions matter and that we genuinely care about their experiences. This validation fosters a sense of emotional safety and creates an environment where open and honest communication can thrive.

Building Trust: Empathy is a powerful tool for building trust in relationships. When we genuinely understand and validate others' emotions, we create a safe space for them to share their inner thoughts and feelings. This trust allows individuals to be vulnerable and authentic, strengthening the bond between them. Trust is the foundation of strong relationships, and empathy is instrumental in cultivating that trust.

Strengthened Communication: Empathy enhances communication by promoting active listening and understanding. When we empathize, we listen attentively to others' experiences and perspectives, seeking to grasp the emotions underlying their words. This deep listening helps us respond with empathy and compassion, leading to more effective and meaningful communication. It fosters an atmosphere where individuals feel comfortable expressing themselves and where conflicts can be resolved with empathy and understanding.

Conflict Resolution: Empathy plays a vital role in resolving conflicts and disagreements. By understanding and empathizing with others' emotions, we can approach conflicts with compassion and seek collaborative solutions. Empathy helps us de-escalate conflicts, find common ground, and work towards mutually beneficial outcomes. It allows us to consider different perspectives and find creative solutions that address the underlying emotional needs of all parties involved.

Strengthened Emotional Connection: When we empathize with others, we connect with them on a deeper emotional level. Empathy bridges the gap between individuals, fostering a shared understanding and emotional connection. This connection strengthens relationships and creates a sense of belonging and support. It helps individuals feel less alone in their experiences, knowing that someone genuinely cares and empathizes with them.

Increased Emotional Intelligence: Engaging in empathetic understanding of others' emotions also enhances our own emotional intelligence. By regularly practicing empathy, we develop a greater awareness of the range of human emotions and a deeper understanding of their impact on individuals. This heightened emotional intelligence improves our ability to navigate our own emotions and respond effectively to the emotions of others.

In summary, empathy and understanding others' emotions are crucial for fostering deeper connections and improving relationships. By validating others' emotions, building trust, enhancing communication, resolving conflicts, and strengthening emotional connections, empathy creates an environment of empathy, understanding, and support. Cultivating empathy allows us to connect with others on a profound level, fostering meaningful relationships built on compassion, understanding, and mutual respect.

CHAPTER 8

THE ROLE OF EMOTIONS IN DECISION-MAKING

The role of emotions in decision-making is a fascinating and complex topic that has been studied extensively in the fields of psychology, neuroscience, and behavioral economics. Emotions play a significant role in shaping our choices and decision-making processes, often exerting a powerful influence on the outcomes.

Emotional Bias: Emotions can introduce biases into decision-making. For example, fear can lead to risk aversion, causing individuals to avoid potentially beneficial opportunities. On the other hand, excitement or overconfidence can lead to excessive risk-taking.

Intuitive Decision-Making: Emotions can facilitate intuitive decision-making, allowing us to make quick judgments based on gut feelings or instinct. These decisions can be valuable when there is limited time or information available. Emotions provide a shorthand way of processing information and guiding decisions.

Value Attribution: Emotions help us assign value to different options and outcomes. Positive emotions can increase the perceived value of a particular choice, while negative emotions can decrease it. Emotionally charged experiences can influence our preferences and the weighting of different decision factors.

Emotional Regulation: Emotions also play a role in regulating decision-making. When faced with difficult choices or conflicting options, emotions can guide us towards considering personal values, long-term consequences, and ethical considerations. Emotions can act as signals, highlighting important aspects to consider before making a decision.

Social Influence: Emotions are contagious and can spread through social interactions. In group decision-making, emotional states can influence the choices made by individuals, leading to consensus or conformity. Emotional contagion can affect both positive and negative emotions, shaping the decision outcomes in a collective setting.

Decision Reversal: Emotions can sometimes lead to decision reversals or regret. For instance, after making a decision, individuals may experience post-decisional regret due to the emotional impact of the outcome. Emotions can influence how we evaluate our choices and the satisfaction or dissatisfaction we feel after making a decision.

It is important to note that the impact of emotions on decision-making can vary across individuals and contexts. Some individuals may be more influenced by their emotions, while others may rely more on rational deliberation. Additionally, the specific emotions experienced and their intensity can also affect decision outcomes.

Understanding the role of emotions in decision-making can have practical implications in various areas, such as marketing, economics, and public policy. By considering emotional factors, decision-makers can design strategies to better align with human behavior and preferences, leading to more effective and satisfying outcomes.

CHAPTER 9

EMOTIONAL WELL-BEING AND RESILIENCE

Emotional well-being and resilience play crucial roles in navigating life's challenges and setbacks. They are interconnected aspects of our mental and emotional health that enable us to adapt, cope, and thrive in the face of adversity. Let's delve deeper into their importance and how they contribute to our overall well-being.

Emotional well-being refers to the state of being emotionally and mentally healthy. It encompasses a range of factors, including emotional awareness, self-acceptance, self-care, and the ability to manage stress and emotions effectively. When we prioritize our emotional well-being, we develop a strong foundation for resilience.

Resilience, on the other hand, is the capacity to bounce back from difficulties, overcome obstacles, and maintain a positive outlook in the face of adversity. It involves the ability to adapt to change, manage stress, and recover from setbacks or traumas. Resilience is not about avoiding or denying difficult emotions; instead, it's about embracing them and finding healthy ways to cope and move forward.

Here are some reasons why emotional well-being and resilience are essential in navigating life's challenges and setbacks:

Coping with stress: Life is filled with stressful events, such as work pressures, relationship issues, or financial difficulties. Emotional well-being and resilience provide us with the tools to cope with stress effectively. By understanding and managing our emotions, we can find healthy ways to navigate challenging situations without being overwhelmed.

Adapting to change: Change is inevitable in life, and it can be both exciting and unsettling. Emotional well-being and resilience help us adapt to new circumstances and face unexpected challenges with greater ease. They enable us to adjust our mindset, embrace change, and find opportunities for growth and learning.

Building relationships: Emotional well-being and resilience contribute to the quality of our relationships. When we are emotionally healthy, we can communicate effectively, empathize with others, and maintain healthier boundaries. Resilience allows us to navigate conflicts and setbacks in relationships, fostering greater understanding, trust, and connection.

Overcoming setbacks: Setbacks and failures are an inherent part of life. Emotional well-being and resilience help us bounce back from disappointments and setbacks. They provide us with the resilience to learn from failures, persevere, and maintain a positive outlook. Resilient individuals are more likely to view setbacks as temporary and find the strength to try again.

Mental health and well-being: Emotional well-being is closely tied to mental health. Prioritizing emotional well-being and developing resilience can protect us against mental health challenges, such as anxiety and depression. By fostering emotional resilience, we can better manage our mental health and seek support when needed.

Developing emotional well-being and resilience requires practice, self-reflection, and self-care. Here are some strategies to cultivate these qualities:

Self-awareness: Pay attention to your emotions, thoughts, and reactions. Practice mindfulness and self-reflection to understand your emotional patterns and triggers.

Building a support network: Surround yourself with supportive and positive people who uplift you during challenging times. Seek help and guidance from trusted friends, family, or professionals when needed.

Healthy coping mechanisms: Identify healthy ways to cope with stress and difficult emotions.